STECK-VAUGHN

PORTRAIT OF AMERICA

Montana

Steck-Vaughn Company

Executive Editor	Diane Sharpe
Senior Editor	Martin S. Saiewitz
Design Manager	Pamela Heaney
Photo Editor	Margie Foster
Electronic Cover Graphics	Alan Klemp

Proof Positive/Farrowlyne Associates, Inc.
Program Editorial, Revision Development, Design, and Production

Consultant: Victor A. Bjornberg, Travel Montana

Published by Raintree Steck-Vaughn Publishers, an imprint of Steck-Vaughn Company.

A Turner Educational Services, Inc. book. Based on the Portrait of America television series by R. E. (Ted) Turner.

Cover Photo: Mountains by © Michael Reagan.

Library of Congress Cataloging-in-Publication Data

Thompson, Kathleen.
    Montana / Kathleen Thompson.
       p.   cm. — (Portrait of America)
    "Based on the Portrait of America television series"—T.p. verso.
    "A Turner book."
    Includes index.
    ISBN 0-8114-7346-5 (library binding).—ISBN 0-8114-7452-6 (softcover)
    1. Montana (State)—Juvenile literature. [1. Montana (State)]
I. Title. II. Series: Thompson, Kathleen. Portrait of America.
F731.3.T49 1996
978.6—dc20   95-25726
                                           CIP
                                           AC

Printed and Bound in the United States of America

4 5 6 7 8 9 10 WZ 03 02 01 00

Acknowledgments
The publishers wish to thank the following for permission to reproduce photographs:
P. 7 © Michael Reagan; p. 8 Big Hole National Battlefield, National Park Service/Jock Whitworth; p. 10 (left) L. A. Huffman/Coffrin's Old West Gallery, Inc., (right) Montana Historical Society; p. 11 Montana Historical Society; pp. 12, 13 Coffrin's Old West Gallery, Inc.; p. 14 Montana Historical Society; p. 15 © Dennis Sanders/Hardin Photo; p. 16 (both) Montana Historical Society; p. 17 Museum of the Rockies, Montana State University; p. 19 Anaconda Deer Lodge Historical Society; p. 20 Montana Historical Society; p. 21 Courtesy Sylvia Duvall; p. 22 © Michael Reagan; p. 24 (top) Big Sky Ski and Summer Resort, (bottom) U.S. Forest Service, Flathead National Forest; p. 25 (top) Montana Travel Promotion, (bottom) Montana Grain Growers Association; p. 26 © D. C. Conklin/The Montana Power Company; p. 27 Rocky Mountain Log Homes; p. 28 Jensen Photos; p. 29 © Chuck Trinder; p. 30 © Michael Reagan; p. 32 Montana Historical Society; p. 33 (top) Montana Historical Society/Mackay Collection, (bottom) © W. A. Simons Files; p. 34 (top) © Donnie Sexton/Giant Springs Heritage State Park, (bottom) © Michael Reagan; p. 35 (top) U.S. Forest Service, Flathead National Forest, (bottom) © Allen Russell/Profiles West; p. 36 © Michael Reagan; p. 37 (both) © Michael Reagan; pp. 38, 39, 40, 41 Glacier National Park, National Park Service; p. 42 © Allen Russell/Profiles West; p. 44 Glacier National Park, National Park Service; p. 46 One Mile Up; p. 47 (top both) Montana Travel Promotion, (bottom) One Mile Up.

STECK-VAUGHN
PORTRAIT OF AMERICA

Montana

Kathleen Thompson

A Turner Book

RSVP
RAINTREE
STECK-VAUGHN
PUBLISHERS
The Steck-Vaughn Company

Austin, Texas

ROCKY MOUNTAINS

GLACIER NATIONAL PARK

Milk River

Scobey

Kalispell

Browning • Shelby • Havre

Clark Fork River

Missoula

Missouri River

Fort Peck Lake

Great Falls

Lewistown

Yellowstone River

GRANT-KOHRS RANCH NATIONAL HISTORIC SITE

HELENA

Miles City

GREAT PLAINS

Anaconda

Big Timber

Billings

LITTLE BIGHORN BATTLEFIELD NATIONAL MONUMENT

Butte

Bozeman

Bighorn River

Livingston

Granite Peak

BIGHORN CANYON

Montana

Contents

Introduction

Some people call Montana "The Big Sky Country." They're talking about eastern Montana where wide, flat plains and rolling hills lead to a seemingly endless horizon of sky. Other people call Montana "The Land of Shining Mountains." These people are looking west toward the Rocky Mountains, where glistening snow tops the highest peaks of more than fifty mountain ranges. "The Treasure State" is Montana's other name. The state earned this name because of its treasured reserves of gold, silver, and copper. Whatever you might call it, Montana is a majestic state of rich resources and spectacular beauty.

Quiet beauty and open spaces are part of the experience of living in Montana.

Montana

From the Plains to the Rockies

Before the arrival of the Spanish in the early fifteenth century, Native Americans in present-day Montana hunted on foot. Those that lived on the plains—the eastern two thirds of the region—were also farmers. These groups included the Blackfeet, the Assiniboine, the Crow, the Cheyenne, and the Gros Ventre. They grew beans, corn, squash, and tobacco. These Native Americans hunted buffalo by stampeding the animals over a high cliff. The hunters then collected the buffalo from the base of the cliff and dragged them to the village.

Other Native American groups living in present-day Montana lived in the Rocky Mountain area in the west. These included the Flathead, Kalispel, Kootenai, and Shoshone groups. They hunted deer, fished, and gathered nuts and other food from the forests.

As the Spanish traveled throughout the Southwest and the Great Plains, they traded horses for buffalo hides, jewelry, and other goods. Between 1600 and

This photo shows the Nez Percé camp at Big Hole National Battlefield in Wisdom, Montana. The Nez Percé fought federal troops here in 1877 while attempting to reach freedom across the Canadian border.

1770, the horse population had spread, and Native Americans had adapted the horse to their own use.

Perhaps the Native Americans most greatly affected by the addition of the horse were those living on the plains. Horses allowed them to hunt buffalo over a large area. Instead of being restricted to living near rivers or streams to grow crops, the Native Americans of the plains became nomads. They lived in temporary villages and followed the migrations of the buffalo. They gave up farming altogether. The Native Americans living in the Rocky Mountains also became more reliant on the buffalo. They traveled to the plains to hunt buffalo and afterward returned to their homes in the mountains.

There was no European settlement in present-day Montana during this time. Except, perhaps, for a few fur traders, the area was left entirely to the Native American population. In 1803 the United States purchased the Louisiana Territory from France for

$15 million. The Louisiana Territory included the land west of the Mississippi River to the Rocky Mountains. President Thomas Jefferson appointed Meriwether Lewis and William Clark to map the new territory. In 1805 the Lewis and Clark expedition reached present-day Montana. As the explorers moved through the region, they gave names to places such as the Marias River and Gates of the Mountains.

In 1807 Manuel Lisa opened the first trading post on the Bighorn River. Many traders who came to the area represented British and American fur companies. The companies hired hunters and trappers to bring in pelts. These trappers sold their furs at an annual gathering called a *rendezvous* and bought supplies for the coming year.

Missionaries also came to the region. Their intention was to convert the Native Americans to Christianity. In 1841 Father Pierre De Smet established St. Mary's Mission, the first permanent settlement in Montana, on the Bitterroot River. Six years

This painting by Charles M. Russell shows an encounter between Native Americans and the explorers Lewis and Clark.

later, the American Fur Company established Fort Benton, on the Missouri River.

Throughout the 1840s, settlers and trappers traded with Native Americans. Trappers and Native Americans traded furs for goods such as utensils and guns. As contact between the groups increased, Native Americans caught infectious diseases for which they had no natural resistance. Thousands of Native Americans died from smallpox and cholera.

In 1846 Great Britain and the United States agreed upon the boundary line between Canada and the United States. Now only Americans could trap for furs in the Montana region.

Three years later gold was discovered in the hills of California, and thousands of miners rushed to the West Coast to seek their fortune. Towns and businesses sprouted up seemingly overnight in California. As a result the federal government and the railroad companies arranged for eastern railroads to connect to the West. To make land available for the railroad, the government set up treaties with the Assiniboine and other groups, removing them to reservations. By 1857 railroad companies were laying rail lines through Montana. The railroads allowed businesses in the East to ship their goods to towns and cities along the railways in the West. The railroad also brought settlers into the region

Two cultures clash in Montana: a teepee is pitched alongside a railroad track.

This photograph shows the lodge of Native American leader Two Moons at Lame Deer, Montana.

faster. The Blackfeet and the Sioux fought these developments—and the settlers—for the next twenty years.

In 1852 gold was discovered in the lower Deer Lodge Valley. Ten years later John White struck a large deposit of gold at Grasshopper Creek, later called Bannack. The rush to Montana was on. In 1863 there were gold strikes in Alder Gulch, which is now Virginia City. In one year the area produced over ten million dollars worth of gold! More gold was discovered in Grizzly Gulch, Confederate Gulch, Rattlesnake Gulch, and Last Chance Gulch, which became Helena.

Towns were established very quickly. Prospectors could dig enough gold to make a fortune—and lose it all in one night at gambling houses in the mining towns. Disputes about the boundary lines between claims were often solved with guns. Outlaws stole shipments of gold from stagecoaches. There was no law and order. In fact, one of the most famous outlaw gangs was headed by Henry Plummer, the sheriff of Bannack. Finally, law-abiding citizens of Montana hired "Vigilance Committees," or vigilantes. When the

This 1882 photo shows a young Cheyenne girl in traditional dress.

vigilantes apprehended someone, there were no trials, courts, or judges to determine guilt or innocence. Often the result was a hanging. Henry Plummer was one of the people whom the vigilantes hanged.

In 1863 present-day Montana and Wyoming were part of Idaho Territory. In 1864 Congress established Montana Territory. The capital was Bannack, but it was moved to Virginia City the next year.

In 1866 Nelson Story drove the first cattle herd from Texas to the Montana Territory. The cattle ranching industry developed soon after. The plains were a good place to raise cattle. The settlers there provided a market for some of the beef. The rest were taken to Cheyenne in Wyoming Territory and shipped to eastern cities. In 1883 the Northern Pacific Railroad was built through Montana Territory, which helped the cattle industry to grow faster.

Settlers and ranchers demanded more space for towns and ranches. They began to encroach upon the land that had been given to the Native Americans in treaties. In the 1870s Native American warriors fought back. They stole cattle and horses and attacked wagon trains and settlements. The United States cavalry was ordered to protect the settlers. In Montana Territory three cavalry regiments were engaged in fighting the combined forces of the Sioux, the Cheyenne, and the Arapaho. The Seventh Regiment was led by Lieutenant Colonel George Custer. In June 1876 Custer underestimated the number of warriors he faced. His mistake was fatal. In the Battle of Little Bighorn, Custer and all two hundred of his men were killed.

The massacre caused a national outcry for revenge. The federal government brought even more soldiers against the Native Americans. By 1880 the Native American wars in Montana were over. So was the Native American way of life. The buffalo were almost exterminated. With their food source gone, over a quarter of the Blackfoot died of starvation. One after another, all Native American groups were removed to reservations.

The end of the fighting encouraged more people to settle in Montana. Most were miners hoping to find gold and silver. In 1881 Marcus Daly was searching for silver near the town of Butte. Instead he found one of the largest copper deposits in the world. Butte Hill became known as the "Richest Hill on Earth," and the camp became another boomtown. Daly built the town of Anaconda on the site. He also founded the Anaconda Mining Company and the world's largest smelter to process the ore. William Clark and F. "Fritz" Augustus Heinze also opened copper mines. The men were so successful that they were soon called the Copper Kings.

During the 1890s the Copper Kings fought each other for political power in Montana. They bought newspapers and they bribed judges and state legislators. Just before his death in 1900, Daly sold Anaconda Mining Company to Standard Oil. This powerful oil company already had large investments in lumber and other Montana industries. Standard Oil became even stronger in

These markers show the graves of the cavalrymen who died at the Battle of Little Bighorn.

The first oil well in Montana went up at Cat Creek in central Montana.

Montana when it acquired the other two copper kings' mining companies.

In 1889 Congress accepted Montana as the forty-first state in the Union. Between 1880 and 1890, the population of Montana grew from 39,159 to 142,924. Homesteaders moved into the state to grow wheat, oats, and other crops. Millions of acres were soon converted to farmland. A good climate with abundant rain ensured good yields.

In 1914 Montana gave women the right to vote—five years before the Nineteenth Amendment to the United States Constitution gave that right to all American women. In 1916 Montana elected Jeannette Rankin to the United States House of Representatives. She was the first woman ever elected to Congress. Rankin served two terms: 1917–1919 and 1941–1943. She worked hard for peace. Rankin voted against the United States entering World War I, and she

Montana's early farmers used horse-drawn plows to break through the prairie grasses.

was the only member of the House of Representatives to vote against entering World War II.

The United States entered World War I in 1917. Montana mining industries prospered because their metals were needed for the war effort. Montana wheat fed the soldiers overseas. In 1918 a drought fell upon the state that continued for several years. Crops failed, and winds blew away the dry topsoil. Montana's farmers studied how to deal with Montana's periodic droughts. They planted different kinds of crops, used irrigation to supplement the rain, and grew drought-resistant types of wheat. By 1929 Montana's farms were fully recovered.

In 1916 Montana elected Jeannette Rankin to the United States House of Representatives. Rankin also served from 1941 to 1943.

In the 1930s the entire country was financially devastated by the Great Depression. Many banks and businesses closed. People lost their savings and their jobs. There was no demand for Montana's products. Then drought hit the region again. Even with the new farm methods, high hot winds again blew topsoil away. Farm harvests dried in the fields. People left Montana in droves. Sometimes they abandoned whole towns.

In 1932 Franklin D. Roosevelt was elected President on the promise that he would solve the nation's economic problems. In Montana that meant starting huge government programs in irrigation, soil conservation, and pest control, as well as providing electricity for rural areas. These projects put many people in Montana to work.

In 1941 the United States entered World War II. The war created a tremendous demand for Montana's copper and coal, which were used to build weapons and to fuel factories. There was also greater demand for Montana's beef and wheat to feed the soldiers overseas. When the war ended in 1945, people began moving to the cities. By the early 1950s, more people lived in Montana's cities than in its rural areas.

The state continued to develop its natural resources in the 1950s and 1960s. New roads brought tourists to Montana, and the state began building parks and historic sites. Private developers opened dude ranches and ski centers. The Yellowtail Dam on the Bighorn River was completed in 1966, and in 1967 construction began on the Libby Dam on the Kootenai River. These projects provided Montana with added electrical power and irrigation.

In the 1970s Montana's economy was given a boost when a worldwide energy shortage created a demand for the state's petroleum and coal. In 1972 Montana adopted a new constitution that emphasized the need for a clean and healthful environment. The constitution also prohibited discrimination on the basis of race. It set a goal to preserve the cultures of Montana's Native Americans.

Most coal mining projects in Montana were strip mines. Instead of digging a mine shaft, a company simply stripped the land. First, it removed all of the trees. Then, it removed the soil, layer by layer, to uncover the coal. After the coal was removed, the land was left useless. By 1973 strip mining for coal became so

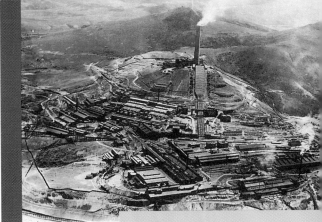

extensive that the people of Montana passed legislation for what was called a "coal severance tax." This law taxed the profits from coal taken from Montana's mines. It set aside the money to reclaim strip-mined land and to help pay for roads, schools, and other services.

In the 1980s fuel prices fell. Farmers also faced drought and low prices for their crops. Worst of all, Anaconda closed all its copper mines and smelters in Montana, causing thousands of workers to lose their jobs. Other mining companies began using modern technology, turning many workers' tasks over to machines.

Today, about 47 percent of the population continues to live outside of urban areas. Montana is constantly looking for ways to help new businesses get started, especially in small communities. One way this is being done is through community development. One company called DoubleTree loans or gives grant money to small communities to open businesses in which many of the residents will be employed. Another company called Montana Private Capital Network invests in new small businesses throughout the state. Small businesses today can operate in rural communities almost as easily as in urban office buildings. That's because modern business is often conducted by computers and fax machines. One main requirement for new businesses in Montana is the same for all residents: that they take advantage of Montana's natural riches without harming its environment.

The Anaconda copper smelter was built in the late 1800s. For 75 years Anaconda was so important to the state's economy that Montanans usually referred to it as "the Company."

The Bald-Headed Prairie

Try to imagine a world without cars, electricity, or running water. Only a hundred years ago, those things were rare or didn't even exist. Settlers who moved onto the Montana plains had very hard lives. That's why stories like this one are important. They teach us about the way things used to be.

Sylvia Duvall was only six years old when her family moved to the Montana prairie in the early 1900s. It wasn't an easy life. "To me," she said, "it was a bald-headed prairie and it was heartless. It didn't have a school-house. It didn't have any roads. The poor livestock didn't have any trees to stand under. I just couldn't get over

it." It was hard for other settlers, too. Montana didn't look anything like the East, the Midwest, or the South. There were no forests, just miles and miles of prairie.

Sylvia's home was typical for a homestead family. It had only one room, which measured about 8 feet by 10 feet. That's probably smaller than today's average bedroom. Sylvia remembers that house well. "There was just barely enough room to set a chair. The bed hung on the wall on hinges and at night you would put it down to go to bed."

There were good things, too. Sylvia's father's land was fertile, and the crops were good. But that didn't last. The weather changed. "One year we were hailed out. Next year we were hopped out—by the grasshoppers.

This fence was eventually covered over during the dust storms that swept across the Great Plains in the 1930s.

In this photo from 1929, Sylvia and Earl Duvall are shown with their first automobile.

And the third year we was blowed out. . . . The dirt was so high in fence lines and . . . around the buildings! And driving, the horses'd . . . just get on their knees and cough."

Drought had come to the prairie. With no rain, the wheat crop shriveled in the fields. The weather was so dry that one time Sylvia had to search forty acres to get enough feed to fill just one washtub! Most of the neighbors moved away. "We had kind of a farewell party for the last two families. . . . When I got home, I just . . . sat on the porch and cried."

But Sylvia Duvall is one of those people who thrives on hardships. She stayed on the prairie and married Earl Duvall, who farmed near her home. Years later she watched her children and grandchildren take over the farm. And what did she think about that bald-headed prairie after all those years? "I have no regrets. I wish I could live it all over again—even to come out to that homestead shack. I wouldn't set and pout and cry because I didn't have my own bedroom. . . . I can't see a life anywhere else that'd have been as good and as free."

Riches Out of the Land

Montana is called "The Treasure State" because mining minerals such as gold, silver, and copper has been an important part of Montana's economy for many years. New things are happening in Montana's economy today, and much of it still has to do with the land.

For instance, the tourist industry is healthier than ever before. In the early 1990s, more than 6 million people traveled to Montana and spent more than one billion dollars a year. It's easy to see why. With the Plains to the east and the Rocky Mountains to the west, Montana is an incredibly beautiful state. Its colorful history of Native Americans, gold mines, and cattle drives helps attract people who want to stand in the places where historical characters stood.

People who are part of the tourist economy are part of the service industry. Service industries are those in which people don't manufacture an actual product. Instead they may work in a restaurant or in a hotel.

This newborn calf and its mother are part of Montana's dairy industry.

Skiing at Big Sky is only one of the tourist activities that are so important to Montana's economy.

Part of a forest ranger's job is to help tourists find where they're going. Tourism contributes more than one billion dollars to the state's economy each year.

They may rent skis at a mountain resort or set a cast for an unfortunate skier. The service industry includes many types of businesses.

Service industries make up about 74 percent of the total economy in Montana. Banks, financial centers, and real estate offices make up the largest part of Montana's service industry. The second largest part is community services, such as hospitals, telemarketers, and car rental agencies.

The next largest part of the service industry is retail trade, which is selling products to people, and wholesale trade, which is selling products to stores that sell products to people. This category includes businesses such as grocery stores, pharmacies, shoe stores, and even toy shops.

The government is also part of the service industry. This doesn't just mean a mayor or a governor. Government services also include fire and police departments, schools, and military bases. The government economy also includes people who work for the Bureau of Indian Affairs, forest rangers, and even the people who work at the missile base near Great Falls or collect fees from tourists who visit Glacier National Park.

Transportation, communication, and utilities are the last category in the service economy. These businesses are crucial to Montana's economy because they include trucking companies, railroads, and companies that maintain oil and natural gas pipelines. Without these services, Montana's goods would never get to market.

Livestock accounts for half of Montana's farm income.

After services, agriculture is the most important part of Montana's economy. Agriculture brings in more than $1.6 billion every year. There are two categories in this group: crops and livestock. Over two thirds of the land in Montana is dedicated to either farming or ranching. Agriculture is an uncertain business because it is affected by so many things that no one can control. There's either too much rain or not enough, or the growing season is too hot or too cold. Also, prices that farmers get for their products are not controlled by the farmers. The prices are controlled by the wholesalers who set the price according to demand for the product. Lower prices for their farm products and uncertain weather have hurt Montana's farmers many times over the years.

Livestock and livestock products provide Montana's economy with more than eight hundred million dollars every year. Some of the largest cattle ranches in the country are found in Montana, so it isn't surprising that the biggest percentage of livestock income is in cattle. Dairy products also are part of livestock income, as are pigs and sheep. The main crop grown in Montana is wheat, but Montana farmers also grow other crops, such as barley, sugar beets, and hay.

Two farmers drive harvesters across some of Montana's wheat fields. Wheat is Montana's most important crop.

A mining crane is used to clear away the land at an open-pit coal mine.

At one time mining—especially copper—was the most important industry in Montana. Today, Montana's biggest copper mines and smelters are closed. The state's copper mines simply couldn't compete with less expensive mines outside the United States. Precious metals, such as gold, silver, and platinum, make up the biggest portion of Montana's mining income now. Most of these mines are in the southwestern part of the state. Petroleum is next in importance, but the price of oil is so low that the industry isn't growing. There is still demand for Montana's coal, too. Most of the work is now done by machines, however, so coal mining doesn't increase employment.

Manufacturing in Montana consists mostly of processing its natural resources. In the lumber industry, for instance, sawmills process trees into boards for construction or into pulp for paper products. Some companies in Montana produce wood products, from pencils to telephone poles. Food-processing factories around the state refine sugar from sugar beets and mill flour from wheat. They also pack meat, process milk, and bottle soft drinks. Other plants process the ore from Montana mines.

There are small businesses that produce miscellaneous products. Some of these are very successful.

A&S Tribal Industries, located in the Fort Peck Reservation of the Assiniboine and the Sioux, is the largest industrial manufacturing employer in Montana. Recently, Missoula, Bozeman, and Butte have become the homes for new companies that specialize in lasers, biotechnology, and environmental cleanup.

For a long time, the people in Montana were dependent on only mining and agriculture. That led to both very good and very bad economic times in the state. Now many other businesses are important to Montana, and the state wants to continue that pattern. In 1985 Montana set up the Science and Technology Alliance, an agency for finding new uses for the state's abundant raw materials. In 1992 the state created the Montana Futures Project to try to make long-range plans for the state. There's much creative energy at work in Montana finding new ways to create more jobs for people.

Logging is a major part of Montana's economy.

A New Way of Life

A&S Tribal Industries is an important business in Montana. It started small in 1974. By the mid-1990s, it was the largest industrial manufacturing employer in Montana, employing about five hundred people and earning approximately $20 to $25 million per year. The A&S in its name stands for Assiniboine and Sioux, the two groups of Native Americans that live on the Fort Peck Reservation in northeastern Montana.

The Assiniboine and the Sioux were forced off their land and onto reservations in the 1800s. Those reservations were established on land that ranchers, miners, and settlers thought was worthless.

Kenneth Ryan, chairman of A&S, expressed the attitudes of his people when he said, "It would be to our benefit to always remember what has happened to us. And we can all work to make sure that something like this never happens again, to any race of people. But nevertheless, bitterness is an emotion which serves no purpose."

Kenneth Ryan and four previous tribal chairmen celebrate the 1987 Fort Peck Assiniboine and Sioux Centennial.

A worker at A&S Tribal Industries works on environmental netting.

As it turned out, the reservations in Montana were very valuable indeed. The land contains oil, coal, and natural gas. The Assiniboine and the Sioux teamed up to raise money for an oil well, and then they began drilling. From the money they made from the oil, the groups established A&S Industries.

Today A&S creates two main types of products. One is fabricated metal products, which are made of pressed and molded metal, such as filing cabinets or storage containers. The other is environmental netting. This material is used to cover pits containing dangerous materials that come from refining oil and other mining by-products. For instance, the United States Fish and Wildlife Service hired A&S to construct a net to go over an oil-refuse pit. The pit was near a wildlife refuge, and the net prevented migrating birds from landing in the pit. If they had, the birds would have died.

The Assiniboine and the Sioux have made a new beginning in the land of their ancestors. While they hold to the traditions of the past, they have shown that they can mold their own future. As Kenneth Ryan explains, "It is the only way to go, to be self-reliant, because it means you are captain of your own destiny."

Art in the Big Sky Country

Two things affect Montana's culture—its size and its population. Montana is the country's fourth-largest state. Only Alaska, Texas, and California have more land. But Montana ranks forty-fourth in terms of population. Only six states have fewer people. In addition, most of Montana's citizens live in urban areas. But even the cities are small compared to many, such as New York or Los Angeles.

Because Montana's citizens live on such a wide expanse of land, Montana's culture emphasizes the wide-open spaces. Montana is "Big Sky Country." In fact, that's the name of the best-known novel about Montana. Called *The Big Sky*, it was written by one of Montana's best writers, A. B. Guthrie, Jr. It tells about the lives of Native Americans and European trappers during the 1820s and 1830s.

Most of the organized cultural activities in the state are in its cities, such as Bozeman, Helena, Missoula, and Billings. These cities have orchestras and groups that present plays, art exhibits, and other

Montana's vastness and variety of terrain is the reason the state is known for its outdoor lifestyle.

activities. Throughout the state, local organizations promote the arts—not only painting, music, and dance, but also drama and literature. These activities are often helped by the Montana Arts Council and the Montana Institute of the Arts. Often small towns can't afford to support cultural activities on their own. It's harder for artists to sponsor exhibits, concerts, and workshops. The council and the institute provide a way.

Montana's museums are located in its cities, but even they emphasize the state's open spaces and its Wild West past. The Museum of the Rockies, in Bozeman, and the Museum of Mining, in Butte, explore the state's geography. Other museums such as the Museum of the Plains Indians in Browning portray Montana's Native Americans. The wars between Native Americans and the newcomers are the subject of museums at the Little Bighorn Battlefield National Monument and the Big Hole National Battlefield.

In Helena the Montana Historical Society honors the past. But it also pays special attention to Montana's great artist, Charles Russell. Russell was a hunter and cowboy in Montana in the late 1800s. His paintings portray scenes from the West, such as cowboys around a campfire, a Native American on horseback braving the winter wind, or a cattle stampede. Russell's paintings are found in museums around the world.

Fine arts aren't the only culture in Montana's cities and towns. In the 1980s, for instance, the people found a special way to usher in the Christmas season— a Christmas Stroll. The strolls began in Bozeman. The

In his novel *The Big Sky,* writer A. B. Guthrie, Jr., celebrated Montana's openness.

city holds an all-day celebration around December 1. Individuals dress in old-fashioned costumes. There are games and competitions. Late in the afternoon, Santa Claus leads the stroll—an informal parade through town. As he passes under street decorations, he tosses glitter into the air, and the decorations light up. As the parade continues, one business

Charles M. Russell's paintings are full of careful detail. This is just one section of his painting called "Laugh Kills Lonesome."

after another turns on its Christmas decorations. The event is a good beginning for the holidays, and it builds a sense of community. Bozeman's stroll has been a model for many other Montana communities.

Montana's heritage has shaped its culture. One example is its parks and festivals. Pictograph Cave State Park preserves the pictographs of the earliest people in the region. The hunting strategy of the Late Hunters is preserved in buffalo "jump sites" in the state. One of them, Wahkpa Chu'gn near Havre, is

Missoula's historic Wilma Theatre shows how important entertainment was to Montana's earliest pioneers.

These children, dressed in traditional oufits, are waiting to perform in a powwow dance competition.

listed on the National Register of Historic Places. About 48,000 Native Americans live on Montana's seven reservations or in its cities. Various groups host powwows all during the year. These festivals feature music, dance, and Native American food.

Montana's history is celebrated throughout the state. Historic markers show the route traveled by Meriwether Lewis and William Clark. Along the way is Pompey's Pillar, a massive sandstone pillar named after Sacajawea's infant son. Lewis and Clark were the first Europeans to see present-day Giant Springs State Park, which has one of the largest freshwater springs in the United States.

The Red Lodge Mountain Man Rendezvous reenacts the days of the trappers in the Rockies. A restored fur-trading post is located at Fort Union, near the junction of the Yellowstone and the Missouri rivers.

The days of the gold rush are celebrated in places such as Bannack State Park. Today, there's a carefully preserved ghost town where the very first gold strike in Montana took place. Cattle ranchers came to Montana in the 1860s, and life on the Plains is reenacted at the

Grant-Kohrs Ranch National Historic Site. This ranch is a working ranch, with activities that demonstrate early ranching ways. Old Montana Prison shows what happened to "bad guys" in Montana. This was the first territorial prison in the West, even though on the outside it looks more like a castle than a jail!

The most important part of Montana's culture isn't its past or even its arts. Montana is special because of its plains, mountains, canyons, rivers, and lakes. Montana has 2 national parks, 10 national forests, 44 state parks, 7 state forests, and 8 million acres of land managed by the U.S. Bureau of Land Management. There are 16,000 miles of fishing streams and 217,000 acres of lakes. Montana encourages its citizens and visitors to spend a lot of time outdoors.

A sample of Montana's open spaces shows what Montana means to its citizens. Along the edge of the Bighorn Canyon is the Pryor Mountain Wild Horse Range, which is home to about 180 wild horses. Rock climbers can find good sites everywhere in the Rocky Mountains, but Humbug Spires may be the most challenging. Fishers cast their lines in the trout streams or Flathead Lake, the largest natural freshwater lake west of the Mississippi River.

One way to tell if the environment is important to people is if they are willing to preserve it. People in Montana have shown their feelings when they decided to restrict strip mining and other harmful practices. The natural beauty of Montana is important to its people. In Montana they have made their values a part of their lifestyle.

above. Whitewater rafting attracts tourists to Montana.

below. This child is skiing in a cross-country race. Cross-country skiing was brought to the United States by people from Scandinavia, where it is a practical way to get around in the winter.

The Prairie Symphonette

It may be hard for people who don't live in Montana to imagine living there. Many of its towns are small and far apart. For example, Scobey is a small town in the northeast corner of the state. The town has a population of about twelve hundred people. You might expect a town this size to have one or two small musical groups. But Scobey is different. It has its own symphony orchestra called the Prairie Symphonette!

The 35 or so members of the Prairie Symphonette aren't professional musicians. Their ages range from 12 to 80. Most are farmers, a few are school teachers, and some are students. Jack Reiner helped start the orchestra and plays the cello in it. He also teaches classes for students who want to play string instruments, such as the violin or the cello. The nearest school with a regular string class is in Billings, about 340 miles away.

But people don't have to be professional musicians to be dedicated to their craft. No one in the Prairie Symphonette gets paid. Ed Retzer, the director, drives seventy miles to conduct the symphony, and he doesn't get paid, either. The concerts include a wide variety of music, from classical pieces, such as Stravinsky's *Firebird Suite* and Beethoven's *Egmont's Overture,* to popular music from the Beach Boys.

Jack Reiner helped found the Prairie Symphonette.

What amazes these amateur musicians the most is that people from four counties come to hear them play. Some drive as far as 55 miles to get to the Scobey school auditorium, where the concerts are held. "People come for reasons I sometimes wonder about. If they'll clap their hands, you know, you don't really care too much about why they're doing it. You're pumped up." After all, what musician is going to complain if people clap when he or she finishes playing?

The Prairie Symphonette obviously brings a lot of satisfaction to the people who play in it. It seems to bring a lot of enjoyment to the people who hear it, too. Why did it happen in Montana? Jack Reiner has one explanation. He thinks it has to do with Montana's open spaces. "This is a country of such openness, it opens the mind too. It's easy to have an accelerated imagination and vision, and that's all we're talking about here; it's just a crazy vision."

The Prairie Symphonette may never play in a fine concert hall. But these performances are done for love, not for fame.

Although their performances are held indoors, the musicians in the Prairie Symphonette enjoy the outdoors.

Glacier National Park

You might not know it, but there's a treasure in northwestern Montana. It can't be measured in dollars, and you can't pick it up and carry it away with you. But if you find it, you'll take away an experience that will last a lifetime. Every year two million people do just that. They discover the treasure that is Glacier National Park.

This park is on land that tells a tale of the history of the earth. The Rocky Mountains of Glacier National Park are made up of billion-year-old rock. Some people think of mountains as never-changing. But there are forces that can change the shape of mountains. One such force is an ice cap, a dome of ice that covers a large area of land. The dome can be more than two miles deep. Two or three million years ago, an ice cap formed over the top of the highest areas of the Rockies in Montana. When the ice cap formed, huge rivers of ice flowed down the mountains. These ice rivers are called glaciers. On their way down, they cut into the rocky mountain walls. Soil and

Sixty percent of the excavation needed to build Going-to-the-Sun Road, shown here, was accomplished by tunneling through solid rock with hand tools.

pieces of rock were swept into the ice and flowed down into the valleys. The glaciers moved forward until the weather became warmer. Over hundreds of thousands of years, they melted into icy-cold glacial lakes. In Glacier National Park, you can see the paths the glaciers carved out. They're marked by sharply cut mountain peaks and deep valleys.

38

Glacier National Park opened in 1910 and has been delighting nature lovers ever since. The park is enormous—it covers 1,584 square miles. Within this area are many types of landscape—prairie grasslands, fields of rainbow-colored wildflowers, deep pine forests, snow-capped mountains, and icy rushing waterfalls tumbling from rocky walls. There are even areas so cold and bare that you'll imagine you've wandered into the South Pole.

The variety of environments provides homes to many different kinds of animal and bird populations as well. Some of them live their entire lives within the boundaries of the park, while others roam in and out or migrate through in the autumn and the spring. Visitors sometimes spot gray wolves moving gracefully through the underbrush. The grizzly bear and its cousin the black bear also have made their home in Glacier National

The one-million-acre Glacier National Park joins with Canada's 130,000-acre Waterton Lakes National Park to form the Waterton/Glacier International Peace Park.

Park. Other animals that live in the park include mountain lions, foxes, and lynx. Sure-footed mountain goats and bighorn sheep wander along mountain slopes and ridges. Glacier National Park also is home to a population of bald eagles. This beautiful bird, the national symbol of the United States, is an endangered species. Scientists at Glacier National Park track and chart the comings and goings of bald eagles in an effort to preserve the species.

Glacier National Park is an area that has its own weather, or microclimate. The park is located on the Continental Divide, along the crest of the Rocky Mountains. The Continental Divide is the line that separates the waters that drain eastward toward the Atlantic Ocean from those that flow westward toward the Pacific. The park stands right at the crossroads where Pacific Ocean air currents meet air currents from the Atlantic and Arctic winds from Canada. All these different air currents help create the park's microclimate. In some areas, it can snow at any time of the year. Sometimes snow closes parts of the park in mid-July. When very warm air fronts bump into very cold air fronts,

Beargrass grows in abundance in Glacier National Park.

Glaciers are formed when layer after layer of snow falls and doesn't melt. Eventually the weight of the snow causes the glacier to move slowly—usually less than one foot per day.

the snow sometimes turns thick like paste. Some people say it feels just like cold mashed potatoes.

In the early days of its history, Glacier National Park was so undeveloped that visitors often spent up to a month camping and exploring. Gradually park managers opened up tourist areas and hotels. Trails were built, and maps were drawn. Going-to-the-Sun Road was opened in 1933. This road cuts right through the heart of Glacier National Park. It was built to show off some of the park's most spectacular areas to visitors who could only spend a day or two. Today, Glacier National Park has a system of three hundred miles of roads and seven hundred miles of trails. Visitors can see some amazing things in just one day's drive, but many people still choose to spend a few weeks. After all, once you've discovered a treasure, you might as well stay there and enjoy it.

Planning for the Future

Today Montana is a mixture of the Old West and the New West. There are vast herds of cattle, vast plains of wheat, and mountains towering against the big sky. But gone are the days of cattle rustlers, miners, and wars between settlers and Native Americans. The New West has women running ranches, computer-run industries, and television satellite dishes. What's next?

No one knows for sure what the future will bring. Nevertheless, the people of Montana have decided to think about the best future for their state. They began by setting up the Montana Futures Project. Project organizers held town meetings all over the state to determine the state's goals. The meetings also identified Montana's strengths so that planners could build on them. With that information the people of Montana now can look for ways to shape their future.

The Futures Project came up with several goals and recommendations to reach those goals. First, it identified a safe, clean environment as one of

Protecting the environment is one of the goals established by the residents of Montana for the future of their state.

Industrial development has destroyed much of the bighorn sheep's natural habitat. Protecting the environment is necessary for the welfare of all living things.

Montana's goals. It suggested that the state encourage businesses to come up with new technology to clean up the environment and protect it. Second, the project identified improving the state's educational system as a major goal.

The people of Montana value education, and they know that tomorrow's high-tech workplace will require technical skills. This is a serious challenge in Montana, where people live so far apart, and many schools are very small.

A third goal focused on health care. The project pointed out that the state's small communities often don't have a doctor or a dentist. It recommended that Montana improve its health care system so that it can serve those communities that are spread out across the plains or tucked away in the mountains.

Whether Montana residents accept these recommendations or set other goals, they certainly are thinking very seriously about the future of their state.

Important Historical Events

1700	Many Native American groups live in areas of present-day Montana.
1805	Meriwether Lewis and William Clark reach Montana.
1807	Manuel Lisa establishes a trading post on the Bighorn River.
1810	David Thompson maps northwestern Montana.
1841	Father Pierre De Smet establishes St. Mary's Mission, the first permanent European settlement in Montana.
1846	A treaty between the United States and Canada makes northwestern Montana part of the United States.
1847	Fort Benton is established on the Missouri River.
1852	Gold is discovered at Gold Creek.
1862	A major gold strike is made at Grasshopper Creek.
1863	One of the richest gold mines is found at Alder Gulch.
1864	The Plummer gang is broken up by vigilantes. Mining strikes break out. Congress creates the Montana Territory out of part of the Idaho Territory.
1867	Nelson Story makes the first cattle drive between Texas and Montana.
1876	Lieutenant Colonel George Custer and his troops are killed at the Battle of Little Bighorn.
1881	Marcus Daly begins mining copper at Butte.
1883	The Northern Pacific Railroad enters Montana.
1886	Subzero winter temperatures drive cattle raisers off the open range.

1889	On November 8, Montana becomes the forty-first state.
1899	Marcus Daly sells Anaconda Copper Company to Standard Oil.
1906	F. "Fritz" Augustus Heinze sells his copper holdings to Amalgamated.
1909	The Enlarged Homestead Act is passed, bringing thousands of people into the state.
1910	Glacier National Park is created.
1913	Natural gas is discovered near Glendive.
1914	Montana gives women the right to vote.
1916	Jeannette Rankin is the first woman ever elected to the United States House of Representatives.
1918	The first of a series of droughts hits Montana.
1924	Coal mining begins near Colstrip.
1931	A drought lasting seven years creates the Dust Bowl in Montana and other Great Plains states.
1940	Fort Peck Dam is completed.
1951	The Great Williston Basin oil fields begin production.
1955	Aluminum mining begins in the state.
1966	The Yellowtail Dam on the Bighorn River is completed.
1973	The state legislature passes the Montana Strip Mine Reclamation Act.
1985	Montana sets up the Science and Technology Alliance to find new uses for the state's raw materials.
1988	The worst drought since the 1930s causes the farming areas to be declared a drought disaster area.
1992	The Montana Futures Project is started.

45

The state flag shows the name of the state in yellow letters on a blue background. In the center is the state seal, depicting mountain scenery, forests, and the Great Falls of the Missouri River. These symbolize the abundant natural resources in the state. The plow represents agriculture, and the pick and shovel show mining. The state motto lies below the scene.

Montana Almanac

Nickname. The Treasure State

Capital. Helena

State Bird. Western meadowlark

State Flower. Bitterroot

State Tree. Ponderosa pine

State Motto. *Oro y Plata* (Gold and Silver)

State Song. "Montana"

State Abbreviations. Mont. (traditional); MT (postal)

Statehood. November 8, 1889, the 41st state

Government. Congress: U.S. senators, 2; U.S. representatives, 1. State Legislature: senators, 50; representatives, 100. Counties: 56

Area. 147,047 sq mi (380,849 sq km), 4th in size among the states

Greatest Distances. north/south, 321 mi (517 km); east/west, 559 mi (900 km)

Elevation. Highest: 12,799 ft (3,901 m). Lowest: 1,800 ft (549 m)

Population. 1990 Census: 803,655 (2% increase over 1980), 44th among the states. Density: 5 persons per sq mi (2 persons per sq km). Distribution: 52% urban, 48% rural. 1980 Census: 786,690

Economy. *Agriculture:* beef cattle, hogs, sheep, wheat, sugar beets, barley, oats. *Manufacturing:* lumber and wood products, petroleum products, processed foods, primary metals, farm machinery. *Mining:* petroleum, coal, copper, gold, silver, natural gas

State Bird: Western meadowlark

State Flower: Bitterroot

Annual Events

★ Central Montana Winter Carnival in Lewistown (January)

★ Copper Cup Regatta in Polson (July)

★ North American Indian Days in Browning (July)

★ Yellowstone River Float, from Livingston to Billings (July)

★ Midland Empire Fair and Rodeo in Billings (August)

★ Flathead International Balloon Festival in Flathead Valley (October)

Places to Visit

★ Alder Gulch, near Virginia City

★ Fort Peck Dam and Reservoir, near Glasgow

★ Glacier National Park

★ Great Falls of the Missouri River, near Great Falls

★ Little Bighorn Battlefield National Monument, near Billings

★ Madison Canyon Earthquake Area

★ Museum of the Plains Indians, near Browning

★ National Bison Range, near Moiese

★ Virginia City, near Dillon

State Seal

Index